SWIMMER IN THE RAIN

Books by Robert Wallace

This Various World and Other Poems (1957)
Views from a Ferris Wheel (1965)
Ungainly Things (1968)
Critters (1978)
Swimmer in the Rain (1979)

SWIMMER
IN THE
RAIN

Robert Wallace

Carnegie-Mellon University Press
Pittsburgh and London

Acknowledgments

Many of these poems, sometimes in slightly different versions, first
appeared in periodicals, to whose editors I make grateful acknowledgment:

THE ATLANTIC MONTHLY: "Everything Comes Eventually." COMMON-
WEAL: "More Than There Is." COUNTER/MEASURES: "The Poet Is
Audited," "Tulip." THE DENVER QUARTERLY: "Story Of A Marriage,"
"Apartment Hunting," "I Go On Talking To You." HARPER'S MAGAZINE:
"The Dictionary Gerrymander," "The Place." HIRAM POETRY REVIEW:
"August: Decline and Fall," "Malveira Da Serra," "The Pretty Lady I'm In Love
With." MICHIGAN QUARTERLY REVIEW: "Does The Stone Know Its
Shape?" THE NATION: "North On Interstate 71," "Driving By" (under the
title "The Ball Field Lights.") THE NEW REPUBLIC: "The Dictionary
Tyrannosaur," "Overcoat," "The Secret Beyond The Ridge," "Swimmer In
The Rain." THE NEW SALT CREEK READER: "Cedric's Poem," "The Other
Island." THE NEW YORK TIMES: "The Girl Writing Her English Paper,"
"Myth, Commerce, And Coffee On United Flight #622 From Cleveland To
Norfolk," "Summer On The Great Plains." OPEN PLACES: "Poetry." PATCH-
WORK: "Death Is Pure White" (under the title "Solid And Plain.") POETRY
NORTHWEST: "In One Place," "Love Poem: Nine Years Later," "The Monday-
Banner," "Experimental" (under the title "Directions For Not Having Faith.")
POETRY NOW: "Bird Theater," "Dog's Song," "Girl In An Apartment
Window." POETS ON: "Another Self." THE SATURDAY REVIEW: "Com-
passes." THE SOUTHERN REVIEW: "Terning," "Sea Turtles" (under the
title "Snappers"), "Starfish." THREE RIVERS POETRY JOURNAL: "A
Fresco Of Swans And Bears," "God's Wonderful Drowning Machine." THE
VIRGINIA QUARTERLY REVIEW: "Don't" (under the title "How Not To
Write A Poem: Don't.") WCLV CLEVELAND GUIDE: "Delicate."

Library of Congress Catalog Card Number 78-74989
ISBN 0-915604-56-6
ISBN 0-915604-57-4 pbk.

Copyright © 1968, 1969, 1970, 1971, 1972, 1973, 1974, 1975, 1976, 1977,
1978, 1979 by Robert Wallace

Printed and bound in the United States of America
First Edition

The publication of this book is supported by grants from the National Endowment for the Arts in
Washington, D.C., a Federal Agency, and from the Pennsylvania Council on the Arts.

For Maggie
—old friend, old friend

CONTENTS

DON'T

Don't go with a girl walking
    in the mountains,
        before the snow is

off the logging roads.
    Even
        if it is March, half green and wet,

blue bells
    in places the sun
        gets at

and molten snow
    in glass ropes pulling everywhere
        and hurtling in

the stream beside the trail.
    Don't
        stand with her

at the top of the falls,
    looking
        down the narrow, pine-locked

valley, where,
    past the first pool
        the water

tumbles to, fluting
    dashing on rocks,
        a dozen

smaller pools,
    greener,
        stiller, lead from falls

to falls amid the trees.
    Above all, don't
        notice

the current draw
     her beagle-puppy
          somehow

to the falls' lip, and over,
     down
          the braiding

roll-top of shattering
     crystal—
          if you do, don't

see him looking up
     to the two of you,
          scrabbling, flap-eared

in the long descent.
     Don't, then,
          run sliding down

tripping on fallen
     pines, and
          boulders in the snow,

nor hunt,
     wet-sneakered,
          shouting, breath frosty

with running, in the empty woods.
     Don't,
          afterwards,

promise to write a poem.

If you do,
     trees will light up
          as green as ever

as the years go by.
        You'll hear the girl
            is married,

then that she has a child
        and is
            happy or unhappy,

it doesn't matter.
        What's there
            to say of a dog's

death,
        a tiny loper
            lost

in the everlasting pines?
        You'll climb
            how many times alone

to the little tree
        on the bluff, in sun
            above

the falls, the valley
        blue with snow.
            Truth is, except for you,

it doesn't matter.
        You talk
            to dogs.

We gave up
        at the rusty iron bridge
            the stream

slides under
        meandering
            out into a field. Dusk

came in a shadow
    of mountains;
        we climbed back up,

chilled,
    still calling, searching
        secret edges

where brush had caught,
    and snow.
        The girl will cry, driving

home. And you'll want
    to promise her
        a poem.

Better to make love
    to her,
        touch her, until she sleeps,

or marry her,
    or anything.
        In a strange city, later,

the moon a silver plum,
    it comes to nothing.
        The poem

was to make it matter, but
    poems can't,
        or only for a moment can—

oh, only for that moment, looking up!
    in time's
        clear

torrent half way down.

I

The sky is July blue. A laughing gull
like a wooden toy, black head, white body, wings
just dipped in shadow, tilting, credible,
slides overhead motionlessly on strings.

IN ONE PLACE

        —something
holds up two or three leaves
the first year,

        and climbs
and branches, summer
by summer,

        till birds
in it don't remember
it wasn't there.

COMPASSES

Gulls on the sand bar
like needles
all point into the nor'easter.

In the pasture, cows
together
put rumps to the wind and rain.

SEA TURTLES

By the end of June
tides bring them up the bay,
on into the channels
that wind through the marsh,
riding the flood,
the females—snouts like sticks,
watchful, ready to submerge.

Like stones with wings
they swim, coasting the shallows,
then lumber
out of wet and mud,
up the sand, above the tide-line,
through reeds or bayberry,
crossing roads if need be, climbing,
clacking and hissing at dogs,
not to be deflected.

And they dig with slow
scoops of their leathery back pads,
left, painfully, then right,
bottle-shaped holes in the sand,
and lay their eggs,
which finally, dusty and deliberate,
dancing heavily,
they cover with angel strokes.

You'll see them
again on the out-going tides,
borne on the pouring emerald,
queens,
lonely, buoyant, clear-eyed,
having done
all the seasons require.

TERNING

Afternoons, on the dock-rail next door,
two Arctic terns, feeding.
Same size, same grays
and flat black caps, same wax-red beaks,
same stumpy, wax-red legs
like carrier jets;
but one does all the diving
into the swirling, green marsh creek—

mother and fledgling, then,
the fat chick bolting the minnows
she catches for him.
She poises, head down, beak to tail in a line,
plunges in the running tide,
then fluttering backwards into the air
backs up to the dock-rail
as if on a string.
Over and over.
ek-ek-ek-EK-ek-ek, says the chick,
gulping shiners.
He points himself, but never dives.

DELICATE

A piece of skim milk moon,
blue of summer sky still visible
through it,
begins at four o'clock to fix itself

above the dunes, shacks, poles
east of our mud creek.
Farther is open ocean, live and sucking.
What's there to do

with such a moon? The gull
stretching his wings settles on a piling;
nobody is surprised.
But you'll remember it

on one of the long, cold, snowy, dreary
days after Christmas,
like an artifact of some lost civilization,
like something fine in a museum.

THE OTHER ISLAND

We lived at the end of an island.
Nights, walking the dog,
we watched the bridge,
a silent arch of lights to the next island,

its green toll booth, the occasional
red taillights gliding up and dropping away,
and the lights over there.
We never went.

Better, we told ourselves,
holding each other,
the lights back through the bayberry
that we know.

The dog ran ahead on the sand, out and back.

AUGUST: DECLINE AND FALL

Early, in lemon sun
the pastel houses sweeten the far shore
like laundry.

A music of sparrows on the clear air
sounds and resounds,
and a mud-hen click-clicks in the marsh.

Big as wedding cakes,
two white launches between water and sky
march down the bay.

Residents are out or coming out
onto their docks,
eyes filling with the expensive morning.

Even after the Empire
collapsed, the beautiful weather went on
for years and years.

THE GIRL WRITING HER ENGLISH PAPER

lies on one hip by the fire,
blond, in jeans.

The wreckage of her labor, elegant as Eden
or petals from a tree,
surrounds her—

a little farm, smoke rising from the ashtray,
book, notebooks, papers, fields;
a poem's furrows.

If the lights were to go out suddenly,
stars would be overhead,
their light come in.

A FRESCO OF SWANS AND BEARS

The moon is a furnace,
sun
a stormy mirror.

Thin vines of smoke
trail
under the starry rafters.

The story always has another
ending.
Night. The salty rose.

CEDRIC'S POEM

A dog who has lived
    with a poet
        for fourteen years

should have a poem.
    He's in
        poems, lying in grass

or loping down a road
    in Virginia
        ten years back.

That's not the same,
    though. And
        don't worry

how good it is
    or try to get everything in.
        Save that.

Just so it's
    a poem a dog can use.
        Allude

to Argus maybe.
    Although
        he sometimes stumbles

on walks, or pees
    like a puppy
        without lifting a leg

(as if his life were a film
    running
        backwards), he's still

the same guy.
    Call
        him now, he'll come.

So this,
    with love,
        is Cedric's poem.

TULIP

It digs the air with green blades,
scooping, curled,
then thrusts out colored gear
in the upper-world

to tap sun and bees and suck
such fuels down
as run its dark machinery
without sound.

BIRD THEATER

At first light
the housecat sits in the window
watching—sparrows mostly,
finches, a jay,
in the various, long leaves of the peach.

Sometimes the mockingbird
with his bag of songs.

Shadowy and musical,
anticipating the peach-colored sun,
they chitter
and hop from limb to limb
in a pageant hours long and fine.

Some have come great distances
to perform for him.

DRIVING BY

On August nights,
in little towns you sometimes see
from the throughways
bloom

the ball field lights—
domes
of smoky brilliance:
brighter than daylight colors,

figures through wire-mesh on the green,
figures in the plank stands,
a tiny moon
dropping out toward left.

They stay
much as we left them—
lichen of the blue American nights
from which we come.

THE PRETTY LADY I'M IN LOVE WITH

takes matches from
the matchbook, not from right
to left nor left to right,
but choosily, leaving
odd
designs—rows of sunny
roses or marigolds, hatted
ladies in a café window,
guardsmen tall
in hot, red busbies on noon parade,
a tiny stage, maybe
the final act of *Hamlet*.
Anything.
Designer lollypops, or conversational
groups by Giacometti,
pilings with gulls,
teeth, fenceposts, poplars, a wig shop,
or candles
gay for something.
A sort of tropical
firing squad, she pots them one
by one, beneath the awning.
Oh, it's the damnedest
thing—you end up doing it, too.

MYTH, COMMERCE, AND COFFEE ON UNITED FLIGHT #622 FROM CLEVELAND TO NORFOLK

Clouds, like bird-tracked snow,
spread to dawn-sun five miles below,

while businessmen (& poets) flow
on air streams, to and fro.

Now, of course, we know
Icarus could have made a go,

formed Attic Airways Co.,
expanded, advertised, and so

have carried Homer and Sappho
from Athens to Ilo

on reading tours—with, below,
clouds spread out like bird-tracked snow.

THE POET IS AUDITED

The I.R.S. takes a third of what he earns
and to make certain, audits his returns.

Computers punch; pale agents warily
explore the tropes and figures of his Form C:

"Profit (or Loss) from Business or Professions
(Sole Proprietorships)" and ask for sessions

critical as his reviews. See him now arrive
at the tall glass-and-aluminum Federal hive,

as he must, sole proprietor of his art,
to lay bare the costs of laying bare his heart;

to ride up to the twentieth floor and explain
that to read in Boston he really took a plane

(ticket, cancelled check) or that he tipped a porter
in Chattanooga an unrecorded quarter;

to prove that the books he says he bought, he bought,
ink, paper, ribbons, stamps, and as he ought

keeps itemized receipts, and that he spent
the sums he says he did for phoning, rent—

and only used his "office" at home to write,
never letting his dog sleep there at night.

Suspiciously they eye the meager income,
the sixty dollar royalty he got from

his latest book, the seven for a sonnet
(he doesn't say he worked a whole month on it,

or hopes that it may last until long after
the government's pulled down rafter by rafter).

No fat ten thousands in movie rights for him,
no N.B.A.'s, nothing from Guggenheim.

They're startled how, year by year by year,
he goes along an unprofitable career,

mostly showing losses (not counting hair,
or time, or his depreciating flair).

Proved truthful, purified and free, he descends
still faithful to his not-illegal ends

and by the public fountain, in public sun,
goes off among the poems still unwritten.

THE DICTIONARY GERRYMANDER

This long-necked, mean old political buzzard
—whose note was heard

first in Massachusetts by Governor Gerry—
has a beak of Salisbury,

rump of Lynn, and claws of Salem and Marblehead,
and wings (now flag-drooping) whose spread

can overshadow the state,
a modern political equivalent for Fate.

Now, here, reduced in size,
he has fixed his eyes

across the page on *get, get ahead, get around, get at.*
Skinny, he wants to get fat.

Like the American eagle, a bird of prey,
he doesn't like not to have his way.

THE DICTIONARY TYRANNOSAUR

Once
shaking the earth with his ten tons,

he loomed up twenty feet in air, defiant-
ly prowling amid giant

ferns. Dangling forepaws,
grinding yards of teeth in a jaw as

big as a steam shovel's—loud, voracious,
terror of the late Cretaceous,

the hugest carnivore
ever was. But no more:

extinct now, penned
in ink to the page at the end

of the T's,
here in the Cenozoic he's

only an historical horror,
a maudlin, merely stamp-size roarer—

for whom, now, there's nothing next.
Sic semper tyrannosaurus rex.

THE MONDAY-BANNER

It is dollar-green & so long
it takes nearly everybody to hold
it over their heads and march along under
it.

DOG'S SONG

Ants look up as I trot by
and see me passing through the sky.

II

At the last blue dusk, streetlamps on in the town,
the first star on, and the half-moon pitted and round,
I slip into the cold tide—with it flowing down,
flowing, flowing. And clomp back by the road.

THE SECRET BEYOND THE RIDGE

The pines push upward
each on one leg,
as in a child's drawing.

Even peering, leaning,
only a few
reach the top of the ridge.

The rest press
up behind the leaders,
a green crowd.

Evenings
there is a lot of sighing
among them—

whether because they know
the secret,
or still don't know.

GOD'S WONDERFUL
DROWNING MACHINE

From taxis up on the coast road
eight nuns come down the beach
to see God's wonderful drowning machine.

It sparkles, and is very blue.

Pleasure makes a small disorder
among them, laughing, pointing,
at the very edge of the roar.

Out far, a ship slides up and down.

Then in the dazzling sun they go,
shoes clappering their black bells,
back up to the road and sky.

Gear and wheel, belt, pulley, wave.

MALVEIRA DA SERRA

An ant's shadow monstering
in morning gold
on the whitewashed wall,

we drink coffee in the sun,
on the kitchen steps,
watching kids in smocks

gather in front of the school
down the hill,
beyond the outcrop with two sheep.

To the north, the mountains shoulder
a clear,
dry blue. In the garden

the big green cactus
listens
with electric ears.

EXPERIMENTAL

Choose a maple wing,
dry and gray if you prefer.

Holding it between thumb and forefinger,
with the other thumbnail
split
the casing.

Delicate as spring green, folded,
miniature,
a life waits to unfurl
and journey toward the sun.

You have ruined it.

SUMMER ON THE GREAT PLAINS

Huge silver bison hulk
& lumber along the Interstates;

birds with broken wings flutter
in their rear-view mirrors.

GIRL IN AN APARTMENT WINDOW

At my sink, I'm running
water for coffee.

A Degas lit in brick,
your window

shows you lifting your gown
over your head,

torso, breasts in the light.
You gather

it like a cloud, bend,
vanish, come

back buttoning a shirt,
tossing

hair outside the collar.
Then, other

windows become other poses.
In one you're

by a table, looking down,
cup in hand.

TO J. V. C. (M. L. A., 1973)

I saw you drinking late, cozy, alone,
amid red plush
at Flaming Sally's in the old Blackstone;

and thought of buying you a whiskey sour,
to break the hush
and boredom of that silk and velvet hour.

But I let you sit—for its small use
as courtesy,
and lest you might be toasting your dry muse.

I hope you were not idler than I thought,
on that red settee,
and would have liked the drink I could have bought.

POETRY

"Omissions are not accidents."

                M.M.

It may be a thing
as the sea is, swaying,

huge, and featureless,
of which even pieces

piling and shoving
miss heaven—

have no beaks, no eyes,
or propensity to rise

except in turmoil.
Or it may be, though small,

a self: as a gull
makes a calm

drifting on the roughest
ocean, or as in a wave's trough

sandpipers mark out discipline
in lines

of flight. Why be modest?
It may be blessed

like the osprey with claws
it dares use.

Power that doesn't know what it's doing
isn't dominion;

nor is vastness all.
Initials

may seem a very pair of birds
thrusting heavenwards.

SWIMMER IN THE RAIN

No one but him
seeing the rain
start—a fine scrim
far down the bay,
smoking, advancing
between two grays
till the salt-grass rustles
and the creek's mirror
in which he stands
to his neck, like clothing
cold, green, supple,
begins to ripple.

The drops bounce up,
little fountains
all around him,
swift, momentary—
every drop tossed back
in air atop
its tiny column—
glass balls balancing
upon glass nipples,
lace of dimples,
a stubble of silver
stars, eye-level,
incessant, wild.

White, dripping, tall,
ignoring the rain,
an egret fishes
in the creek's margin,
dips to the minnows'
sky, under which,
undisturbed, steady
as faith the tide pulls.
Mussels hang

like grapes on a piling.
Wet is wet.

The swimmer settles
to the hissing din—
a glass bombardment,
parade of diamonds,
blinks, jacks of light,
wee Brancusi's, chromes
like grease-beads sizzling,
myriad—and swims
slowly, elegantly,
climbing tide's ladder
hand over hand
toward the distant bay.

Hair and eye-brows
streaming, sleek crystal
scarving his throat—
no one but him.

DEATH IS PURE WHITE

At dusk, two egrets
like snow
fish the edge of the marsh creek.

One each of everything
that is,
no more; and nothing a symbol

for anything else. Stilt
legs slide
indolently in the water.

Death is pure white, and hunger
takes long
lovely steps, wading into darkness.

THE PLACE

Where to hide a leaf, he said,
        is in a tree.
A starling in the flock.
        Water in the sea.

In limbs, in waves, in air—
all of them hidden there!

MAGGIE AT NOON

The noon walk is for chasing squirrels.
From the top step

of the English building, she looks out,
pointing,

quivering, and then with utterly Byzantine
care stalks glass-legged

across the leaf- and acorn-littered lawn
and finally rushes—

leaping at the oak from a branch of which
the squirrel now looks down.

She runs and sniffs, re-runs, looks up.
Mostly, in fact,

it's the same fellow, the same tree,
the same zigzag.

How she longs to be red in tooth and claw!
How he squawks!

NORTH ON INTERSTATE 71

At eighty only the very distant
(or the very near) seems real—

intermediate grassbank, river, wood,
and stubble-field blur and go bent

past windshield, dashboard, hand on wheel.
The ridge beyond the next is cloud.

DOES THE STONE KNOW ITS SHAPE?

—or the branch
its thrust in air,
dividing that colorless rock with ore?

In the dark leaves
under the darker leaves, mice
work; in the attic, a runner of moon.

Round and round,
like a record done with music,
turn the Homeric weeds and flowers—

white reefs,
islands, in a midnight drizzle;
dogs trotting along a road in the sun.

III

Amy's off Hatteras—tonight she'll come
on here. All day, all day her swirling skirt
beats at the dune-grass, makes the cedars moan.
Check lines. Lock. Shutter. Hide. Tie down the heart.

LOVE POEM: NINE YEARS LATER

Not Christmas this time, but
just after. Dirty snow
stripping from a dirty city
like weasels vanishing.

The sunlight runs, lemon,
watery. And you are gone,
a mile maybe, hiding
among your friends, considering

a life of your own.
Across the street a fireplug
in a boy's red knit hat
eyes our house.

The traffic moves, or doesn't.
The year runs down.
There is no sparing one another—
love survives

its failing. Dusk
brings a sparrow or two
into the trees, like leaves
until there are leaves.

OVERCOAT

It has lasted through
two wars, five Presidents, a dozen jobs.
And two wives.
It has traveled on three continents.

The oldest thing I own,
it's older than I am.
Spirit aside,
I have long since become what I eat.

Frayed, lining torn, pockets worn, strings
dangling like light
from cuffs and buttonholes,
it bulges and looms. Girls

who weren't even born when I bought it
think of patching us both up.
It may still
last long

enough to go to heaven in—
an empty overcoat waving an empty sleeve,
going off like a severed kite
into the sky.

ANOTHER SELF

We keep trying to find each other
but the landscape changes, you're

three-quarters up and the cliff face
crumbles, or the trees keep moving

between us, the woods become water
and I have to turn away and swim

out to the surface. The girl I'm touching
in this strange room wears your face,

we get nearer, you're one of the paratroopers
floating away from the plane. At the last

moment you see me in the window, but
it's snowing. You've never been to Paris.

I GO ON TALKING TO YOU

We're getting the divorce—
I am, I'm the one who wants to;
you don't, you're reluctant, you merely agree.
But I stand in the door, or at the bottom
of the fire escape
or I come back up the fire escape.
Though it's settled and what I want to do,
I go on talking to you.

Afterwards, too, by myself by the window,
I keep on asking
why, if you love me, you do what you do.
I watch your lights, and argue
my way down through the seven levels
of your history of lies.
The clock shrugs. Almost two.
I go on talking to you.

Maybe keeping on talking is what love does.
It's what I have to do.
Outside his building at five, parked
in the vapor-lights' peachy hue,
in the lull after I know you won't be leaving
now till morning, and you're sleeping
by him (or doing what lovers do),
I go on talking to you.

EVERYTHING COMES EVENTUALLY

As, today, May's shirtsleeve air,
dogs, jonquils, girls,
sunlit past seven o'clock; or

as, in time, the first snow rasping
brown oak leaves.
Love, too. And the end of it.

STORY OF A MARRIAGE

Girls shouldn't marry fathers;
but, in him, she did,
though maybe it was something
she didn't know, or hid

even from herself. He got
what any father gets—
proudly free-hearted love,
rebelliousness, and debts.

As fathers do, he tried
to meet her every want,
and at the same time wished
the straight tree would grow bent.

Twice, in their years, she ran
away with other men,
as daughters do; and twice
in the end came home again.

But now grown up, at last,
she's going off for good.
Her job makes him unneeded;
a new man, misunderstood.

Lucky to have warmed himself
at the bonfire round her bones,
as fathers must he grieves
and wishes her well at once.

APARTMENT HUNTING

A huge yellow cat, maybe a Persian, rose
from the oval bathroom rug
when I opened the door. Loose, more like dry fur
still piled in the shape of a cat,
front paws still tucked under,
as if it had starved
waiting for its owners to remember,
facing the door maybe for years, it rose
and came purring past my legs into the empty rooms.
I don't remember eyes. Tail up.

This was a dream. I have the house,
while you, staying with friends, go apartment hunting.
So was I dreaming your dream,
your new life in the image of our old cat
welcoming you? having waited for years?
Or was it my dream of yours, death
and the impoverishment of empty rooms?
I can, it seems, loving you, wish you ill.

FIGURING IT

In twelve years,
or 4,383 days (counting
three Leap Years),

we must have made
love at least 1,753
times. More

times than Plato says
the just man
is happier than the unjust—

which isn't a
bad way of figuring
it. I

have years before
your other lovers
catch up.

MORE THAN THERE IS

1   Wanting more than there is,
I thin myself to the surface of water,
transparent, reflecting
light, brushing air, keeping
at an even distance from the clouds
and from the crystal, pink, orange, white
pebbles, from the silt, crabs,
sliding starfish, a needle-fish snaking
its fire-hose snout around a clump of mussels—
clear, faintest green,
a lens;
level, easy where I am, or
lifted by the tide, the same; or into waves.

2   The sun plunges west—
the dry, gray dock,
the green creek whirled by a boat's wash
into Queen Anne's lace;
two red-billed skimmers like swooping
fighters in the shadow of a marshy bank.
Gold-leaf, and then moon-foil.
I want more than there is:
a miraculous commotion,
stars over the roof, mirrors, the fine gold hair.

3   At five o'clock, in the first gray light,
a wedge of tiny, fanning ripples
like a feather
wanders on the incoming tide: somebody
struggling. I cup him up, a
half-inch moth, white, gray, and tan

like marbling on an old book,
with delicate crimson antennae.
Flat to my knuckle, he dries out;
flutters to a piling to await the sun.

AFTER THE DIVORCE

1   A new past—shoots of a few leaves
that may grow to saplings, then to trees
around the clearing of the present.

I, too, have a lover now. She
this instant—snoozing in the sun,
in easy reach—makes me happy.
The frames of the present pass, a film
full of the colors of a scene,
the summer salt creek I have known
for fifteen years. I can touch it,
touch her. The odds are I am happy.
But I recall that past when you
through long days by this chill, green creek
were here with me and we were happy,
till the film flickered, broke, and burned.

Flowerpots on your sill, in Cleveland,
cat in the window, drugstore corner
blanching through a summer afternoon.

Begin again. So, *suave est.*

2   Awakened, on the dock, ghostlier
than the skimmer slicing the shadows
of the marsh-bank, I watch the high
tide's molten fullness slow and stop.
It is July again, a clear night.
With rushes of panic I stumble
to the dark boathouse phone and spin,
in the sputterings of a match,

the rage and longing that set off,
over five hundred miles, the phone
in the apartment you keep with him;
and count its ring four times—amazed
that you are real and still exist—
and hang up so you cannot answer.

STARFISH

Where last summer Sam Hocking tossed the clumps
of mussels when he cleaned his floating dock,
the bottom of the salt creek blooms with starfish
big and heavy as hands. They slide and pile,
traveling on a myriad fleshy feelers,
and clutch, feeding, prosperous, beautiful,
eye-spots at the ends of arms sensing the light
shimmering down through silty green. It is
a murderous, a pastoral, scene.

One summer, masked, and watched from holes by eels
and through their lifted claws by crabs, I dove
the velvet-dusky bottom, deeper, picking
tiny, white stars, collecting them by dozens
in a plastic bag—watery constellations
to be dried, hundreds, on a sheet of glass
in hot sun and then glued, quarter-inch Antares,
on homemade Christmas cards. After each dive,
I flippered to the surface, gulping air.

The kids next door, this summer, at low tide
wade in and swoop up tens of horny stars,
spreading them on the dock-boards in the sun,
and watch them dying without thinking that
is what it is, and soon go splashing off
to other games. The starfish stiffen, stink,
long arms awry. I think of the sticky feelers
groping, yearning, clutching at blue sky;
go back to reading *The Spanish Civil War.*

I can't sort out a simple, marshy creek,
confused by kind, by need, by nature of things,

by guilt too easy, innocence too easy.
One of the pilots at Guernica, perhaps,
whose Stuka followed the bombs on down to strafe,
or one of the dead, could say how that differed
from the hot meat of our ordinary dinners,
from starfish, happy kids, and on the dock
an aging, tender-hearted murderer.

IN THE FIRST PLACE

Go on living. The big moon,
a day or so off full, shines
in. It makes a square of light
like white powder on the floor—
bonelight, scoured of its red meat.
It is the sun, reflected.
And on the ceiling of the room,

another square of this light,
dimmer, twice reflected now,
by moon and by the salt creek
runneling below the window,
glimmers. A moving surface
of wave-shadows, dark ripples
like flights of misty, vague birds

passing, passing. Both moon shapes,
which are trapezoids really,
move east, as the moon moves west;
and as the moon sinks, the one
on the carpet stretches and
grows vaguer, and then less white,
smudging the shadow of chair's

leg, of the couch's shoulder.
The one on the ceiling dims,
stretching, too. Is yellower.
And then the moon, orange again,
duskier, sinks to the earth,
goes down. It was time to go
to bed in the first place. Go.

POSTCARD

You came up from the woods with flowers,
and looked them up in a book: Blue
Phlox. So, this was what we knew—
you came up from the woods with flowers.

DREAMS

The soul's home movies,
little explosions

in memory's filerooms,
secrets too dark

for bearing, or tremblings
from the rest of

the iceberg, they
have always been omens,

revelations, tribal
tales and runes, cave, wood,

a ripply mirror
of the waking world.

Unbidden, deepest
truth or deepest lies,

they have the spinster in us
falling, turn our parents

into trees on a tundra,
make the professor

or the wily businessman
a boy locked in a

1935 Plymouth while
his mother shops—

lovely arcana which,
since they exist,

must be somehow true,
though they may be

recollections of events
that never really happened,

places we've never
seen or been, people

who are strangers
all our waking years—

old comedies and
Busby Berkeley films

of grand desires, defeats,
great loves we seem

to have forgotten,
monsters we recall

without the fangs and grimaces,
as they were by day.

Trash of the mind
blown into wild disorders

by the galaxial winds
of sleep? Our true

being, of which the
everyday is only

the tulip's green blades
and colored cup,

the sightless flower?
Maps in cryptogram,

by which we might
find out our unknown selves

if they could ever be
decoded? A dim

and wholly beneficent
healing of the quotidian—

white corpuscles
of the consciousness,

accidentally observed?
Dark bribes and fairy tales

we need to survive?
Candy for despair?

Our most cloaked assassins?
What are they, dreams?

Milky, random constellations
of mind-stuff we

take, deceived, for deepest
omens? Deepest omens?

The late late late show
in which we watch

the story of our lives?
Intercepted transmissions

of the dead? Junk?
Well, still, since they

keep the world a little more
mysterious, though

we may never understand,
they come to be

companions of the descent
each makes alone,

our own bloody nonsense
at least, unstealable,

something, lies or truth,
we can't give away

and, like the history of dinosaurs,
wouldn't be without.

Carnegie-Mellon Poetry

The Living and the Dead, Ann Hayes (1975)

In the Face of Descent, T. Alan Broughton (1975)

The Week the Dirigible Came, Jay Meek (1976)

Full of Lust and Good Usage, Stephen Dunn (1976)

*How I Escaped from the Labyrinth
  and Other Poems*, Philip Dacey (1977)

The Lady from the Dark Green Hills, Jim Hall (1977)

For Luck: Poems 1962-1977, H. L. Van Brunt (1977)

By the Wreckmaster's Cottage, Paula Rankin (1977)

New & Selected Poems, James Bertolino (1978)

The Sun Fetcher, Michael Dennis Browne (1978)

A Circus of Needs, Stephen Dunn (1978)

The Crowd Inside, Elizabeth Libbey (1978)

Paying Back the Sea, Philip Dow (1979)

Swimmer in the Rain, Robert Wallace (1979)

Far From Home, T. Alan Broughton (1979)

The Room Where Summer Ends, Peter Cooley (1979)

No Ordinary World, Mekeel McBride (1979)